To Rose and Matt

A DAY IN THE LIFE OF A
BACKYARD JUMPING SPIDER

JUMPER

JESSICA LANAN

Roaring Brook Press

New York

What if you were very small?
Smaller than a cat or a dog,
a bar of soap,
or a bottle cap.
As small as a bean.

What would your world be like?

That is Jumper's world.

Jumper is hungry and ready to hunt.
She walks along the garden fence. Her
tufted feet let her hook on to its surface.
A line of silk shows where she has been.

Imagine walking not just on the ground but on the walls and ceiling, too. You wouldn't need to be afraid of heights with your own built-in safety line.

That is how Jumper moves.

The corner garden is a jungle, where she can find and stalk her prey. But Jumper also faces dangers of her own . . .

What if you could sense tiny vibrations through your elbows and knees? You wouldn't miss a bug's soft steps, or the rush of beating wings.

That is how Jumper feels.

Jumper hides from the
Carolina chickadee just
in time.

Jumper climbs among the beans. A grasshopper is warming in the sun, and she would make a tasty meal. The grasshopper is big and strong, but Jumper is a gifted hunter.

Can she clear the distance?

What if you could jump five times your body length? You could cross a whole garden without a running start.

That is how Jumper jumps.

But she is not fast enough today.

zzzzzzvvvvvvvvvnnnnnnnnnnr

Down,
down,
Jumper ventures deeper into the
garden, still searching for prey.
Meanwhile, the drone of wings
grows in the distance . . .

You detect sound using tiny hairs in your ears. What if your whole body was covered in these hairs, and you could hear through your arms and legs?

Quiet comes again to the garden.
Jumper walks through plants that
seem tall enough to reach the clouds.
But what will she find to eat?

If you close one eye, the world seems flat. Imagine if you had eight eyes instead of only two. Then you could see in every direction at once . . .

above and behind and all around.

That is how Jumper hears.

She scoots to safety, hidden
from the parasitic wasp.

Footsteps fade away. But now there is something else—a softer buzz from nervous wings. Jumper climbs for a better view. Her keen eyes help her judge the distance. She pulls a safety line of silk and fixes it fast. And when the moment is just right . . .

That is how Jumper sees.

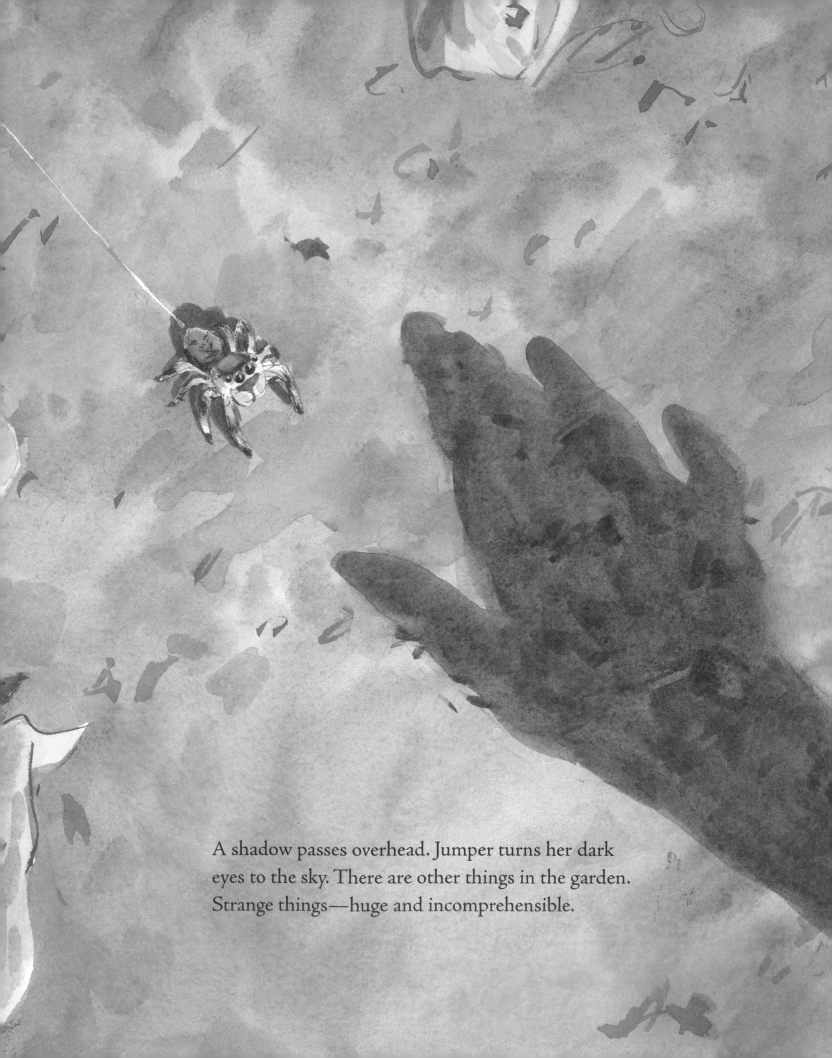

A shadow passes overhead. Jumper turns her dark eyes to the sky. There are other things in the garden. Strange things—huge and incomprehensible.

She JUMPS!

She is a hunter in her garden jungle,
both predator and prey, our small and
stealthy friend and neighbor . . .

Jumper.

HOW DOES JUMPER DO IT?

SPIDER PAWS

A spider's feet are a bit like a cat's paws. Jumping spiders have tufts of hair called *scopulas* and tiny claws that help them grip on to little bumps on almost any surface. This allows them to walk on walls and even upside down.

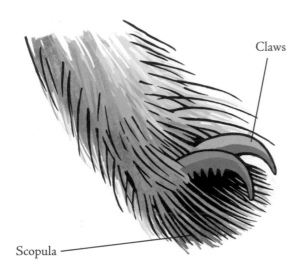

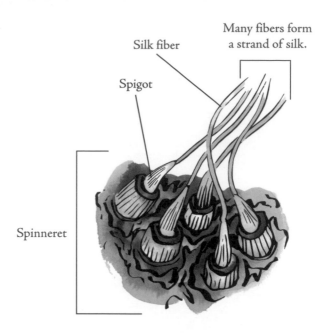

SILK TOUGHER THAN STEEL

Spiders can make up to seven different types of *silk* through their internal silk glands and external organs called *spinnerets*, located at the end of the spider's abdomen. The different types of silk are used for different purposes. Jumping spiders use the toughest type, *major ampullate silk*, for a dragline that they leave wherever they go. This very flexible silk is tougher than steel or even Kevlar!

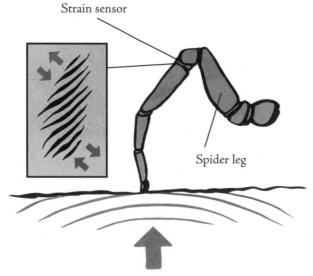

Vibrations disturb the surface beneath the spider.

A WORLD OF VIBRATIONS

Touch is one of the spider's most important senses. Jumping spiders feel vibrations using special sections in their hard exoskeletons called *strain sensors*. These organs are made up of tiny slits that expand and compress when a vibration passes through their leg. The sense of touch is a key element in hunting prey and evading predators. It is also used in spider courtship, when the male spider will tap rhythmically on the ground or rub certain body parts against each other in order to make vibrations to impress the female. Some spider species have thousands of strain sensors on their bodies.

INCOMPARABLE ATHLETES

How do jumping spiders leap so far? The spider uses muscles to compress her *cephalothorax* (head), increasing the pressure of the *hemolymph* (spider blood) inside. When she is ready to leap, valves open to allow the pressurized fluid to rush into her legs. The sudden rush helps to propel the spider forward.

Pressure pushing outward

Pressure released into rear legs

Thanks to this special ability, an average jumping spider can jump more than five times the length of her body, and some jumping spider species have been reported to jump up to twenty times their body length. That would be like an adult human jumping the length of three school buses end to end!

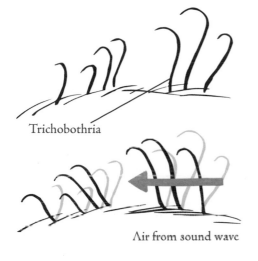

Trichobothria

Air from sound wave

CAN SPIDERS HEAR?

Special hairs called *trichobothria* on the bodies of jumping spiders are sensitive enough to detect sound waves traveling through the air at certain frequencies, particularly those created by a flying wasp's wings. While there is still some debate about the role of spider hearing, one thing is certain: Jumping spiders can hear some sounds just like you can, even though they do not have ears.

EXCEPTIONAL VISION

Despite their size, jumping spiders have better vision than some small mammals. They see the world at a higher frame rate than humans do, which means that a movement that appears smooth to us would look choppy to them. Jumping spiders have four pairs of eyes. The positions of their eyes give them a visual field of nearly 360 degrees. Each pair is slightly different in form and function.

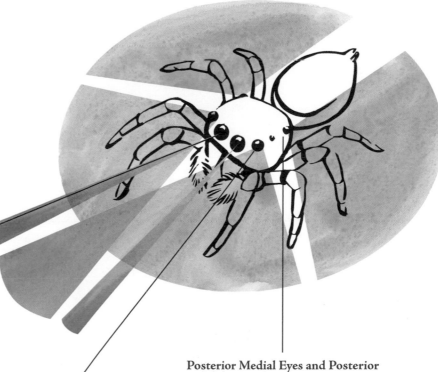

Anterior Medial Eyes (AMEs)

The AMEs are the spider's distinctive, large, forward-facing eyes. They see a narrow view, and the spider can move these two eyes independently. Some jumping spider species can see only a limited range of color with their AMEs, while others can see every color from ultraviolet to red.

Anterior Lateral Eyes (ALEs)

The forward-facing ALEs have a wide visual field and are well adapted for judging distances. They provide *binocular vision*, an overlapping view that helps the spider detect movement and enhances depth perception.

Posterior Medial Eyes and Posterior Lateral Eyes (PMEs and PLEs)

The two pairs of eyes called PMEs and PLEs are positioned on the sides or back of the spider's head. They are lower resolution than the forward-facing eyes and can only detect light in the green, blue, and ultraviolet spectrum.

SPIDERS, SPIDERS EVERYWHERE

Jumping spiders are among the most common predators on planet Earth, found in environments ranging from tropical coasts to mountain peaks, on every continent except Antarctica. As of 2019, Salticidae (the Latin name for the family of jumping spiders) contains more than six thousand named species and counting! Despite their diversity, jumpers share many similar habits.

ANATOMY OF A JUMPING SPIDER

Unlike insects, which have three main body sections, spiders are *arachnids*, with only two: the *abdomen* and the cephalothorax. The two sections are connected by a narrow waist called the *pedicel*.

THE REGAL JUMPER

The spider in this book is a regal jumper (*Phidippus regius*), a common jumping spider in the southeastern United States. Females can be gray, red, or white, with iridescent green or purple *chelicerae* (jaws). Males have striking black-and-white patterns. *Phiddipus regius* spiders are especially common in Florida, but they can also be found as far south as the Caribbean, as far north as Virginia, and as far west as Texas. *Phiddipus regius* is one of the largest jumping spider species in the world. The largest females can grow up to 22 millimeters, or nearly 1 inch! Because of their beautiful colors and relatively large size, *Phiddipus regius* spiders are sometimes bred as pets.

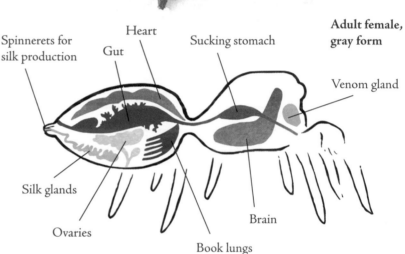

Abdomen   Pedicel   Cephalothorax

Adult female, gray form

Spinnerets for silk production

Gut   Heart   Sucking stomach   Venom gland

Silk glands   Ovaries   Book lungs   Brain

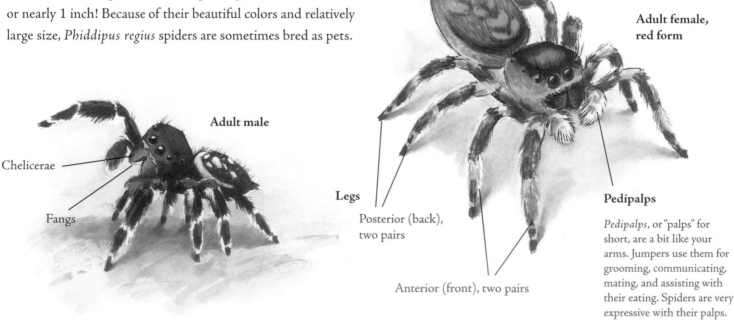

Adult female, red form

Adult male

Chelicerae

Fangs

Legs

Posterior (back), two pairs

Anterior (front), two pairs

Pedipalps

Pedipalps, or "palps" for short, are a bit like your arms. Jumpers use them for grooming, communicating, mating, and assisting with their eating. Spiders are very expressive with their palps.

LIFE CYCLE OF A JUMPING SPIDER

Spiders begin their lives as tiny eggs, which the female lays and wraps carefully in a silk pouch. The babies that emerge are called *spiderlings*. Spiderlings can spin long strands of lightweight silk that, when caught by the wind, will lift the tiny spider into the air. This behavior, called *ballooning*, allows the babies to scatter to new destinations. Once settled, the young spiders begin the important business of hunting, eating, and growing. Many jumping spider species in temperate climates live for just one season, but in some species, the female can survive the winter in a shelter made from silk. Once she has reached her full size, she will mate and the cycle will begin again.

GROWING PAINS

Spiders belong to the group of animals known as *arthropods*, creatures that have an exoskeleton, a segmented body, and paired appendages. The *exoskeleton* is a hard shell that protects the internal organs and provides structure. (You may have seen an exoskeleton on a crab or a lobster.) But, unlike your bones, this shell is stiff and cannot grow. As the spider gets bigger, the shell gets tight, causing spiders to go through a process called *molting*. During this process, the head portion of their exoskeleton comes off and the spider pushes itself through the hole wearing a brand-new, temporarily flexible exoskeleton in a larger size. Most jumping spider species molt five or six times before they become adults. If you look carefully, you might find one of these little leftover shells in your home or garden.

COURTING DANGER

The courtship displays of jumping spiders are elaborate. The male spiders are often very colorful and boast special iridescent hairs called *plumose hairs* that reflect ultraviolet light, making their show spectacular to the eyes of a female jumper. (Even the black-and-white male regal jumpers have bright-hued chelicerae.) They show off their colors and "dance" by moving their legs and pedipalps and by drumming rhythmically on the ground. In some species, the male jumping spiders rub together special structures on their bodies called *files* and *scrapers*. The male spider can use these structures to make sounds and "sing" to the female. The stakes could not be higher: If the female is sufficiently impressed, she will allow the male to mate with her. If not—watch out! He might become her dinner.

GLOSSARY

abdomen: one of the two sections of a spider's body, located behind the cephalothorax

arachnid: an arthropod with eight legs and two body sections; this group includes spiders, scorpions, ticks, and mites

arthropod: an animal with paired appendages, a segmented body, and an exoskeleton; this group includes all arachnids, crustaceans, and insects

ballooning: the dispersal of spiderlings by long strands of silk that can lift them into the air

binocular vision: the ability for two eyes to work together simultaneously to perceive the same three-dimensional object

cephalothorax: the front or "head" part of a spider's body, which holds the brain, eyes, stomach, and legs

chelicera (plural: chelicerae): the jaw of a spider

exoskeleton: an external skeleton that protects an animal and gives its body structure

files and scrapers: structures on a spider's body that the spider uses to make vibrations

hemolymph: spider blood, which is blue in color

major ampullate silk: the toughest type of spider silk, known for its extreme strength and flexibility

molting: the process of shedding an exoskeleton or other covering to replace it with a new one

pedicel: a narrow section of a spider's body that connects the cephalothorax and the abdomen

pedipalps: appendages located near a spider's mouth that are used for grooming, communicating, feeding, and other tasks

plumose hairs: colorful hairs on a male spider's body that are used to impress a female for mating

scopula: a tuft of hair on a spider's foot that helps it hold on to surfaces

silk: a strong fiber made of proteins from inside a spider's body, used for locomotion, protection, shelter, hunting, mating, and caring for young

spiderling: a very young spider

spinneret: the structure on a spider's body where silk is excreted

strain sensor: a structure on a spider's body that can sense vibrations traveling through a surface

trichobothria: specialized hairs on a spider's body that can sense movements in the air

AUTHOR'S NOTE

Many experts, colleagues, and friends helped with the creation of this book. I would especially like to thank Dr. Paul Shamble at Harvard University for his invaluable assistance, encouragement, and feedback. Thank you to Dr. Richard Bradley at Ohio State University for answering my early spider questions, and to Dr. Sebastian Echeverri for his detailed notes on spider vision. I'd also like to recognize the work of Dr. Mostafa Nabawy at the University of Manchester for his excellent photography demonstrating jumping spider locomotion. Finally, I am grateful to Jonathan and Isadora Bruneau for reading and modeling for me, and to Katherine Roy, Elisha Cooper, and Brian Floca for offering support, encouragement, and plenty of distractions along the way.